FASHION

RENNAY CRAATS

Weigl Publishers Inc.

Published by Weigl Publishers Inc.
350 5th Avenue, Suite 3304, PMB 6G
New York, NY 10118-0069
Website: www.weigl.com

391.0097
Cra

Library of Congress Cataloging-in-Publication Data

Craats, Rennay.
 Fashion : USA--past, present, future / Rennay Craats.
    p. cm.
 Includes index.
 ISBN 978-1-59036-972-2 (hard cover : alk. paper) -- ISBN 978-1-59036-973-9 (soft cover : alk. paper)
 1. Fashion--United States--History--Juvenile literature. I. Title.
 GT615.C73 2009
 391.00973--dc22
                        2008023862

Printed in the United States of America
1 2 3 4 5 6 7 8 9 0 12 11 10 09 08

All of the Internet URLs given in the book were valid at the time of publication. However, due to the
dynamic nature of the Internet, some addresses may have changed, or sites may have ceased to exist
since publication. While the author and publisher regret any inconvenience this may cause readers, no
responsibility for any such changes can be accepted by either the author or the publisher.

Weigl acknowledges Getty Images as its primary supplier for this title.

Every reasonable effort has been made to trace ownership and to obtain permission to reprint copyright
material. The publishers would be pleased to have any errors or omissions brought to their attention so
that they may be corrected in subsequent printings.

EDITOR: Heather C. Hudak
DESIGN: Terry Paulhus

Fashion
Contents

Fashion Through the Years   4

2000s   6

1990s   10

1980s   14

1970s   18

1960s   22

1950s   26

1940s   30

1930s   34

1920s   38

1910s   42

1900s   44

Activity   46

Further Research   47

Glossary/Index   48

Fashion
Through The Years

Since the beginning of the 20th century, there have been vast changes in the fashions worn by U.S. citizens. From the glitz and glamour of the 1920s to the no-nonsense work outfits of the 40s and swinging styles of the 60s, the United States has had its finger on the pulse of the fashion world.

Often, fashions are influenced by events in society. World War II inspired simple, **utilitarian** designs. The prosperity of the 1950s caused a rebirth of elegance. The free spirits of the 1960s and 1970s chose to express their **individuality** through patterned, bright fashions.

In some cases, fashion ifluences culture. The beat culture of the 1950s gave broad exposure to American writers. In recent years, the spread of hip-hop style has added a distinct flavor to music, language, and fashions worn today.

The United States continues to be a driving force in the world of fashion. New York is one of four cities in the world thought to be a hub for fashion icons. The buying power of U.S. citizens can influence trends around the world. U.S. designers work tirelessly on the leading edge of style, always looking for the next big trend. Whether the future of fashion will provide more flair or simplicity, the United States will be ready to contribute, scissors and sewing needles in hand.

Fashion
2000s

East Meets West

Starting in the 1990s, traditional Asian culture had a strong influences on fashion. **Asymmetrical** designs, off-center closures, embroidery, bamboo prints, and characters from Asian languages were common in designs by North American and European designers. However, in the early 2000s, these elements of style had filtered down from high fashion to everyday wear. Silk, a fabric often used in many Asian garments, was a popular medium for all types of western attire, from formal to casual wear. Some designers fused silks with more commonplace western fabrics, such as cotton and wool. Men's

Rock Small, Rock Hard

East Meets West

2000s

Rock Small, Rock Hard

In the early 2000s, many people began listening to music produced by bands that were linked to smaller music companies. Often, these companies provide greater creative freedom and allow the musicians to make less commercial music. This new independant, or "indie," music, soon began influencing fashion. Indie fashion typically included business and formalwear, such as sport coats, ties, waistcoats, and scarves, worn with jeans or corduroy pants. Faded and vintage clothing became a staple of the indie community, and many outfits were put together at secondhand and thrift clothing stores. Slip-on and dress shoes became popular, as well as Chuck Taylor sneakers made by Converse. These were originally prized for their low cost, but as they gained popularity, the price of the sneakers quickly increased.

2001

Mademoiselle magazine, in print since 1935, publishes its final issue.

2002

Bright colors, floral patterns, and feminine cuts are common in women's clothing.

fashion designers experimented with an Asian-inspired suit. These suits had high collars, no lapels, and long buttoned closures along the front of the jacket. They were paired with Mandarin-collared shirts that looked like traditional oxford dress shirts without the fold-over collar. Asian influences extended to t-shirts that were printed with Japanese or Chinese lettering.

2000s

Spice Girl to Soccer Mom

Victoria Caroline Beckham entered the public eye as Victoria Adams in 1994, when she joined the pop group Spice Girls. The British media dubbed her Posh Spice, a nickname that has followed her since. In 1998, Victoria married British soccer superstar David Beckham, and after leaving the Spice Girls, she recorded several solo songs. In recent years, however, Victoria has been better known for her involvement in the world of fashion. In 2000, she modeled for London Fashion Week. A year later, she moved to the other side of the runway, designing a line of high-end jeans for Rock & Republic. In 2006, Victoria set out to create her own fashion label, dvb. dvb continued to produce the jeans Victoria had designed for Rock & Republic, but expanded to include fragrances and accessories, such as

sunglasses. Victoria's style has influenced high society on both sides of the Atlantic ocean. In 2007, she moved to Hollywood, becoming a fashion fixture in that community. Women across the United States began to wear

her signature haircut, a short bob that is high in the back, angling to a point over the shoulders. In 2007, Victoria was presented with British Glamour Magazine's awards for Woman of the Year and Entrepreneur of the Year.

**Spice Girl to Soccer Mom
Victoria Beckham**

2003	2004	2005
Plastic shoes called Crocs become a fashion sensation.	Gel bracelets are all the rage.	Preppy clothes make a comeback.

2005

Boho Chic

In 2005, fashion was moving in circles. The bohemian, or "boho," and hippie looks of the 1950s and 1960s returned briefly to **vogue**. Long, tunic-style tops, coin belts, and "floaty" skirts formed the core of a boho outfit. Gilets, a type of short vest with a fur lining, were commonly worn as outwear. Many boho outfits were accessorized with carry-alls called "hobo bags," satchels, or small knapsacks. One of the more popular choices in footwear was the ugg boot. Made from sheepskin, these thick, low-cuffed boots were typically worn with leggings, skirts, or jeans. Between 2005 and 2007, boho chic could be seen at nearly any fashionable gathering. It was often worn by celebrities, such as Sienna Miller and twin sisters Mary Kate and Ashley Olsen.

Boho Chic

2006
The skinny suit becomes popular for men.

2007
Loose-fitting hip-hop styles begin to give way to form-fitting clothes.

2003

J-Lo

J-Lo
Jennifer Lopez

Jennifer Lopez had been a professional actress, singer, and dancer since 1987. She starred in several movies in the late 1990s, including Jack, Money Train, and Selena, for which she received a Golden Globe nomination. It was the release of her first album in 1999, however, that made her a household name. The album, "On the 6," received much praise and nominations for many awards. Jennifer's popularity grew quickly, as she released several successful albums over the next few years. In 2003, Jennifer entered the world of fashion, launching the clothing line JLO by Jennifer Lopez. This fashion line for young women included t-shirts, lingerie, jeans, purses, belts, and other accessories. Jennifer was often praised for her positive body image and influence on younger girls. In addition to her fashion line, Jennifer also released a popular line of fragrances.

Into the Future

The 2000s were the decade of celebrity style, more than any before. As Americans turned to TV and movies in record numbers, the faces on the screen became their guide to fashion. Do you see this as a positive or negative influence on culture? Where do ideas about style come from other than celebrities?

2008

Wide-legged pants are a must-have fashion trend.

2009

2010

Fashion
1990s

made the new sound popular. Fans began dressing in large flannel work shirts worn over T-shirts and baggy, ripped jeans. Comfort was the key, and looking sloppy was a bonus. Considering fans spent a great deal of time "moshing" to the alternative band's music, this focus on comfort made sense. Toward the end of the nineties, people began growing out of grunge. They wanted something a bit more stylish. Glamour was the order of the day. This, too, went along with a music style. Rather than hard rock, swing and jazz bands briefly gained popularity in the U.S. This brought a renewed interest in the styles of the 1920s and 1930s. Women began wearing cocktail dresses out on the town, finishing off the glamorous look with gloves. Men donned linen suits, hats, and wing-tipped shoes when heading out for the evening. The late-nineties looked like a scene out of history—people danced the jitterbug, sipped fancy drinks, and were dressed to the nines.

1990s

Friendly Fashion

The huge success of the sitcom Friends did more than boost network ratings. It influenced the way Americans dressed and styled their hair. Salons from coast to coast were swamped with women wanting the shaggy, layered look of "Rachel" or the shorter bob often worn by "Monica" on the show. "Phoebe" introduced women to sassy hair

From Grunge to Glamour

1990s

From Grunge to Glamour

In the 1990s, America was introduced to "grunge." This style came alongside a new type of music from Seattle, Washington. Nirvana, Pearl Jam, and Soundgarden were some of the grunge bands that

1991

Belly shirts are worn to show off navel piercings.

1992

Grunge becomes a leading fashion trend.

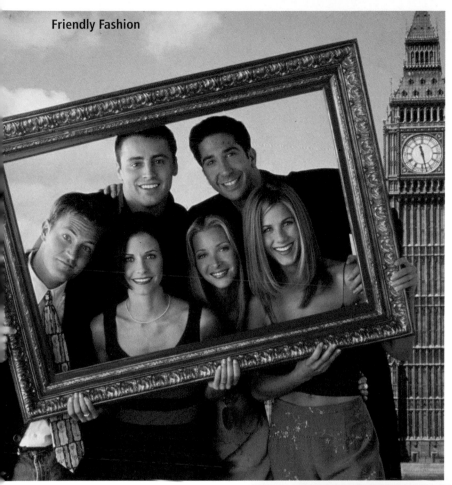

Label Crazy

Fashionable Americans in the 1990s were influenced by brand names. Tommy Hilfiger, Nautica, and GAP were labels that all stylish people needed to have on their clothes. These names were not only on the inside label—they were often splashed across the front of shirts. Designers and stores supported the casual trend of clothing. GAP stores were lined with row upon row of T-shirts and sweatshirts, along with khaki skirts and cargo pants. Tommy Hilfiger fashions, which could be found in large department stores, dressed men and women in upper crust style. The brand names were also attached to popular perfumes and colognes. To dress the part was not enough—Americans had to smell the part as well.

clips and accessories. Actresses had not caused such a fashion stir since Farrah Fawcett's feathered locks in the 1970s. As the seasons passed, the actresses changed their hairstyles, and U.S. women changed along with them. U.S. men also got in on the Friends frenzy. The brushed-forward style worn by "Joey" and the spiky look that "Ross" sported found their way into U.S. salons. The six stars continued to lead the fashion brigade throughout the decade.

Label Crazy

1993
Mondetta sweatshirts gain popularity.

1994
The Gap opens its discount clothing outlet, Old Navy.

1995
IBM scraps its dress code for casual wear.

11

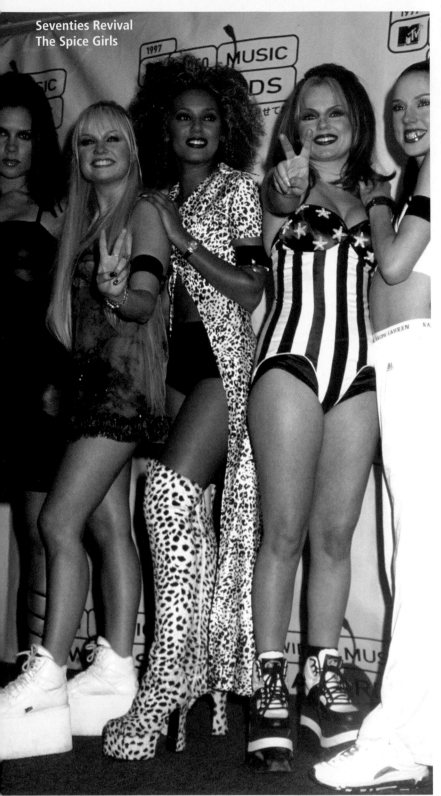

1990s

Seventies Revival

Disco found its way back during the 1990s, at least as far as fashion was concerned. Young people relived a decade they had not even been around to experience the first time. Polyester shirts, of both solid colors and patterns, flew off store racks. Flared jeans, or bell bottoms, were on every teenager's wish list. Many styles had flowers printed or embroidered onto pockets or pant legs. Short shorts, called hot pants, worn with halter tops also returned to women's wardrobes. The seventies revival would not be complete without platform shoes. Girls and women were suddenly three or four inches taller in this footwear. The shoes caused some problems, though. British pop star Baby Spice fell while wearing platform shoes. So did many others. The colors and accessories of the nineties also smacked of the 1970s. Hot pink, burnt orange, and powder blue all came back into fashion. Brown polyester was the choice fabric for pantsuits, jackets, and shirts. To add something extra to these recycled styles, many designers added sequins and glitz. Americans loved this glance to the past and added powder blue eye shadow to make the look authentic.

1996
Happy face shirts and peace sign necklaces make a comeback.

1997
Corduroy pants become commonplace in women's closets.

1998
Cargo pants become a major trend for men and women.

Four Elements of Fashion

Rap musicians had a style all their own in the nineties. Early in the decade, many of these rap stars wore tight-fitting knit caps, chunky jewelry, and expensive brand-name running shoes. Soon, fans began to adopt this way of dressing. U.S. youths began to wear blue jeans that were several sizes too big and hung below the waist. Hooded sweatshirts and baggy shorts were also rap-inspired inner-city fashions. Baseball caps were a must, but they were not worn traditionally. They were cocked to the side or worn backwards. Some hip-hop fans strung chains from their belt loops into their pockets, and the chain was attached to their wallets. Topping off the hip-hop look

was a large jacket with a sport team's logo emblazoned on the back. The Los Angeles Raiders logo was a favorite to wear on hats and jackets. Even young

people who had not listened to the music borrowed some of the styles. Hip-hop or rap musicians continued to influence U.S. fashion throughout the nineties.

Into the Future

Fashion tends to move in cycles. The cuts and styles popular in previous years may be stylish again one day in the future. for examples, 1970s styles were popular in the 1990s, and 1980s styles were common in the 2000s. Think about the clothes people wear today. Can you imagine yourself wearing the clothes your parents wear when you reach their age? What trends do you think will be popular in 5, 10, and 20 years?

1999

Hawai'ian shirts are popular for men.

2000

Fashion designers around the world use the Sydney Olympics to show off their athletic wear.

Fashion
1980s

Superstar Style

Many U.S. style trends have been set by fashion-forward entertainers. In the 1980s, teenage girls were glued to their television sets, memorizing outfits and hairstyles worn by such stars as Madonna. Hair tied with pieces of mesh allowed dark roots to show through dyed blonde locks. Ripped clothes looked like they came from a thrift store, but the designer labels on them made them hot sellers. Eighties fashion was about pushing limits. Teens across the nation showed off their midriffs with half-shirts. They sported lots of make-up, crimped their hair, and even wore underwear as outerwear! To top off the latest look, chunky jewelry, including crucifixes, hung from long necklaces made of beads or fake pearls.

Preppie Power

Yuppies dominated the 1980s. Yuppies, which stands for "young urban professionals," had a great deal of money and were not afraid to spend it on looking good. These successful Americans were doctors, computer technicians, engineers, and entrepreneurs, and their clothing and accessories displayed their income.

Superstar Style
Madonna

1981	1982	1983
Olivia Newton-John sparks a fitness clothing fashion trend.	Japanese designers, such as Issey Miyake, Kenzo, and Hanae Mori are successful in the United States.	Karl Lagerfeld begins designing for Chanel.

Preppie Power

1980s

Dare to Wear Denim

Jeans were originally worn by people who lived and worked in the countryside. Many Americans wore jeans, but few designers had bothered to add denim to their lines. In the 1980s, clothing designers discovered denim. Successful designers, including Calvin Klein and Gloria Vanderbilt, released their identifiable brand-name jeans—the designer's label was visible on the waistband or pocket of the pants. These new jeans were much more expensive than jeans had ever been before, but Americans were willing to pay for the name. Some jeans were pre-torn to give them the fashionably tattered look. The eighties jean fads included stonewashed jeans. These jeans were dark blue with light streaks all over them. They embraced the worn or "washed-out" look that fashion-conscious Americans loved. Some manufacturers even added numerous zippers that had no purpose. Michael Jackson's zippered jackets helped this fad become especially popular.

Women wore pearls as everyday accessories, along with cardigans and long, stylish skirts. Men kept up their flawless appearance with perfectly pressed dress pants and expensive shirts. As the eighties neared an end, so did the popularity of the preppie look. A new craze called grunge took its place and lasted into the nineties.

Dare to Wear Denim

1984
Nike signs a contract with Michael Jordan for the rights to release the Air Jordan sneaker.

1985
First Lady Nancy Reagan packs 19 suitcases for a 10-day trip to Europe.

15

Fitness Fashion

Fitness Fashion

The fitness craze of the eighties and the popularity of disco dance filtered into fashion. Movie stars from *Dirty Dancing*, *Fame*, and *Flashdance* made the look of workout clothing fashionable. Before this decade, only serious dancers wore legwarmers to keep their muscles from tightening up. Now all sorts of people wore them. Legwarmers came in every imaginable color and pattern, and Americans matched them with their outfits. Fashion-aware Americans wore legwarmers over their pants. The 1983 movie *Flashdance* made wearing ripped clothing acceptable. Americans wore big sweatshirts over workout tops. Actor Jennifer Beals brought the casual look to accepting Americans.

A Head for Style

After Tom Cruise wore them in *Risky Business* and Corey Hart sang about them in "Sunglasses at Night," Americans needed the perfect pair of shades. Ray-Ban sunglasses became very popular with both men and women. People wore them indoors and outside. Another important accessory was the headband. In the fitness-crazy decade, headbands or sweatbands became the style. Stars such as John Travolta in *Staying Alive* and

A Head for Style

1986
Levi Strauss & Co. release their Dockers line of slacks.

1987
Nike air soles are popular footwear.

1988
Asymmetrical haircuts are popular with women.

Olivia Newton-John in her "Physical" video made the headband a must. Headbands helped draw attention to the "radical" hairstyles of the eighties. Crimping irons were a necessity for women. This wavy iron produced a kinked effect on hair. Another fad was messy and spiky hairstyles. But they were not easy to achieve. Men and women used a new product called mousse to hold the style they wanted.

1980s

Mimicking Miami

The success of Don Johnson's hit television show *Miami Vice* turned the spotlight on his sense of fashion. His simple and comfortable way of dressing gave men an easy and fun fashion to follow. Trendy men wore light pants with matching jackets, which were worn over pastel T-shirts, rather than button-down dress shirts. Mesh shoes did not require socks. Shaving also was unnecessary. A day's worth of stubble finished off this casual, rugged look.

Mimicking Miami

Into the Future

People had more money to spend on clothes in the 1980s than had in many of the other decades of the 20th century. As a result, they were able to quickly adopt new trends and styles. How important do you think it is to keep up with trends? Which fashion trends cost the most to buy? Why is this?

1989
Calvin Klein Eternity hits the market.

1990
Tie-dyed shirts and hippie fashions gain popularity.

Fashion
1970s

Seventies Fads

1970s

Disco Style

The late seventies were ruled by disco. To stay hip, Americans had to know how to dress. For many, their model was John Travolta, the disco king. He inspired U.S. men to don flashy suits with silky shirts opened to mid-chest to show off the gold chains around their necks. The suit pants had to be bell-bottoms. Disco dancing was best done in a pair of clunky platform shoes. Women's disco-dancing style came from celebrities, too. Many dancers borrowed the look of the Swedish singing sensation ABBA. Women painted powder-blue eye shadow (or shadow

1970s

Seventies Fads

To be truly fashionable in the seventies meant being "hip." Cruising in the car, dressed in the coolest bell-bottoms and platform shoes, was not enough. The seventies fashion plate needed tunes. Eight-track cassettes featuring the best disco hits littered the dashboards of nearly every car. Portable tape players were designed so that people could take their music with them. Walking down the street with a transistor radio was a sign of coolness. By the mid-seventies, the eight-track fad was replaced by cassettes.

1971

The women's retail chain Bebe is founded in San Francisco.

1972

Nike Shoes begins production.

fashioned in a rainbow) on their lids. Some added a string of tiny rhinestones to their eyelids for extra glitz. They also copied ABBA's skin-tight satin pants, matching satin shirts, and high-heeled shoes. Some women preferred off-the-shoulder, loose dresses to dance in. Regardless of the style, many Americans waited eagerly for the weekend, when they could dress up and dance the night away.

Casual Clothing

**Disco Style
ABBA**

1970s

Casual Clothing

The 1970s was an era of easy-going styles. Fashion came from the streets, not from a designer's new line of clothing. Americans wore what was comfortable. High school and college students loved blue jeans and T-shirts. Sleeveless tops and muscle shirts also gained popularity with both men and women. Women embraced the new hip-hugging clothing that showed off their curves. They had fought for equality and expressed this by wearing pants, not dresses, to work and out on the town. Velvet or satin pant suits turned heads in the seventies.

1973
Shorter haircuts gain popularity among women.

1974
Giorgio Armani releases his menswear line.

1975
Foot Locker opens its first store.

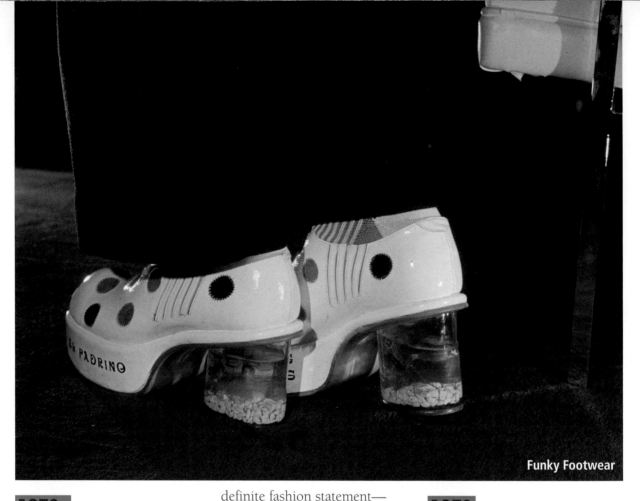

Funky Footwear

1970s

Funky Footwear

What Americans wore on their feet said a great deal about them. Footwear in the seventies was a

definite fashion statement— "I have style." Thick-soled, open-backed shoes called clogs became a hit with both men and women. For those riding the fitness wave, sneakers were the footwear of choice. Sandals and platform shoes became must-haves for fashion-conscious Americans. Some women leaned toward high boots that laced up to the knees. The boots were most often worn with hot pants, which were short shorts. This look had also been popular in the sixties and was carried into the early seventies by disco stars and Hollywood actors.

1970

Saying No to the Midi

In 1970, the calf-length midi dress promised to be "the" style of the year. U.S. women did not agree. They preferred the shorter mini skirts they had grown used to throughout the sixties. Other women were comfortable in jeans or pants. They did not want to buy a new wardrobe every time designers released new styles. To show their feelings, many women kept on dressing the way they had been doing, and they left midi dresses hanging on store racks.

1976
The peasant look is introduced.

1977
Punk rock music and fashion explode in New York.

1978
Velcro is first available for purchase.

Imitating Hair Styles
Dorothy Hamill (center)

Imitating Hair Styles

In 1976, Olympic gold-medalist Dorothy Hamill captivated Americans. Her flawless jumps and spins on the blades of her figure skates brought her international attention. But her haircut brought her fame. Many people tried to imitate the "Hamill wedge." All over the country, women cropped their hair in a bob, just like Dorothy's. Not all women favored the figure skater's hairstyle. Some preferred the Farrah Fawcett look. Fawcett's big, blonde, feathered hair drove women to their hairstylists by the thousands, all trying to capture the breathtaking look of their favorite Charlie's Angel. Farrah Fawcett dolls, posters, and advertisements gave women the chance to study Fawcett's style—and try to copy it. The Hollywood superstar affected fashion sensibility all across the nation.

Into the Future

Today, tools such as the Internet allow people to share ideas about fashion much more easily. Research online to see what people around the world are saying about the latest runway fashions. Which fashions do think will become popular with the general public?

1979
Disco fashions start to fade.

1980
"Big" hairstyles begin to gain popularity.

Fashion
1960s

Flower Power

1960s

Flower Power

In the mid-sixties, the hippie look took hold of the U.S. Beehive hairdos were out and bone-straight hairstyles became the rage. Women even ironed their hair to achieve the straightest style possible. Men and women favored long hair that draped around their faces and down their backs. The "flower power" of the sixties was everywhere. People wore flowers in their hair and painted or embroidered flowers on their shirts and faded bell-bottomed jeans. Skirts that flowed to their feet were an essential part of a female hippie's wardrobe. Shoes were optional, as many hippies preferred to be "at one with nature" and walk around barefoot. Also, these people were the first to wear T-shirts as outerwear, but they went further than that. They tie-dyed the shirts with spirals and splashes of vibrant colors. This style would forever be associated with the peace-and-love generation of the sixties.

1960s

The Beatle Invasion

The Beatles were discovered in a Liverpool pub and became the most popular British musicians in history. In 1964, John Lennon, Paul McCartney, George Harrison, and Ringo Starr invaded North America

1961
Cover Girl makeup is first sold in department stores.

1962
K-Mart opens its doors for business.

1963
Amancio Gaona, owner of many retail clothing brands, including Zara, begins his career.

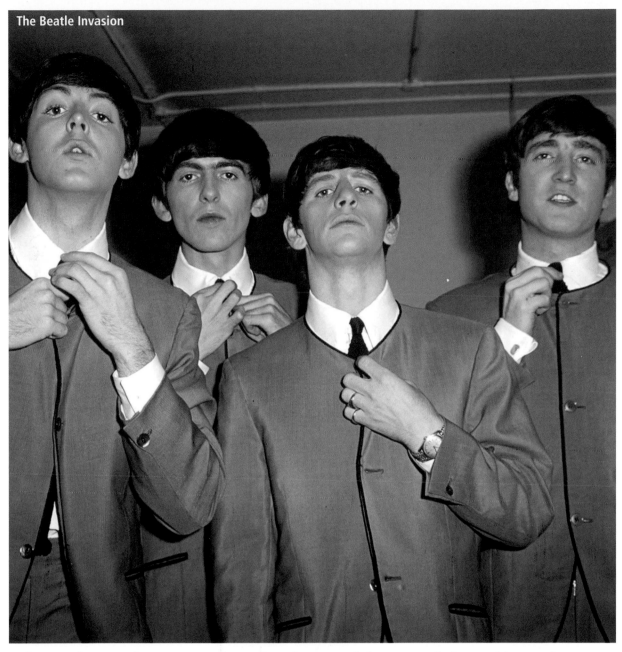

with more than just their remarkable musical talents. They brought their style with them, too. During their U.S. tour, the Beatles, with their unbeatable harmonies and masterfully written songs, appeared on The Ed Sullivan Show. They also sported their signature bowl-cut hairstyles and matching suits. Everywhere they went they were greeted by screaming teenagers. The shaggy hairstyles that fell over their ears swept America as quickly as Beatlemania did. As the sixties rolled on and hippies became popular, the Beatles' image changed, and Americans were eager to keep up with their trendsetting styles. By the time the band broke up in 1970, they had established themselves as rock-and-roll legends.

1964
Mop-top hairstyles are common for men.

1965
Paraphernalia, the first U.S. store to sell clothing in the British "mod" style, opens in New York.

Twiggy Style

Leslie Hornby's classmates called her "Sticks" because of her small frame and boyish figure. Then, at 17 years of age, the British girl captured the attention of the fashion industry. Now called Twiggy, she became the world's first supermodel. She arrived in the U.S. in 1967, where she was met at the airport by flashing cameras and adoring fans. Americans had not seen such a reception since the Beatles invaded earlier in the decade. With her bobbed hair, false eyelashes, and bean-pole, waifish figure, Twiggy became a symbol of innocence and youth. Some were uncomfortable about the 5-foot, 6-inch, 91-pound star representing the ideal look. Still, that would not stop Americans from following her lead. Her trendsetting clothing line could not keep up with the demand for her short dresses, knit tops, and striped stockings. Dolls, lunchboxes, posters, trading cards, and other goods were quickly produced as the Twiggy look swept the country. She retired at the end of the sixties, but not before becoming a fashion icon.

Twiggy Style

1966
Twiggy wins the "Face of the Year" contest, launching her fashion career.

1967
Roland Barthes publishes an in-depth look at language used in the fashion culture.

Short Skirts

In 1965, less really was more. French designer André Courreges sent models onto the runway in high white boots and skirts that rested four inches above the knee. This scandalous design surprised the audience into silence. But not for long. Soon, women cheered for the miniskirt, though often they could not afford it. Then British designer Mary Quant brought runway styles to ordinary people. She not only made her styles more affordable, she also made them shorter. Her stores sold out of the radical new style every day. She sewed all night to keep up with the demand. Courrèges soon realized that there was a market for everyday fashion for women. He made his styles available to anyone daring enough to wear them. Millions of American women did so throughout the rest of the decade.

Short Skirts

Into the Future

The Beatles proved that musicians can have a strong influence on fashion. Disco, hip-hop, punk and heavy metal music also have made certain styles of clothing popular. Think about the music you listen to today. How do the musicians dress? Have they influenced mainstream fashion?

1968
Calvin Klein enters the world of fashion with simple, elegant designs.

1969
Levi Strauss & Co. begin selling bell-bottomed jeans.

1970
The Body Shop is founded in Berkeley, California.

Fashion
1950s

Dressing Up Dresses

Women looked to accessories to dress up their wardrobes. Some young women pasted rhinestones and stick-on pins and brooches on their skin for a different look. This way, even in strapless dresses, their shoulders could glitter and sparkle. For some women, versatility was the answer. Pop-it necklaces were a great way to get many necklaces in one. Women could lengthen or shorten the beaded string by popping it apart and adding or taking out beads. These necklaces could go from waist-long to chokers in a matter of seconds. Other extras, including pearl necklaces, were made popular by television's June Cleaver. Hats, which had been an essential part of a woman's wardrobe in previous years, became less important in the 1950s. However, many women still wore hats and gloves to church or the synagogue. Younger women often decided to go hatless.

1950s

Style Guide

Teen styles were fun in the 1950s. Blue jeans were a must in every American's wardrobe. They were the ultimate piece of casual clothing. During World War II, jeans had been sold only to people employed in defense work. By the fifties, everyone

Dressing Up Dresses

1951	**1952**	**1953**
Short evening dresses become popular for women.	Mascara wands are used for the first time.	Fashion models in San Francisco form a union, demanding a $5 fee for fittings and rehearsals.

wore them. They became U.S. fashion symbols throughout the world. Jeans were often rolled up so that there were thick cuffs at mid-calf length. Another casual style was short shorts, which often had rolled cuffs as well. This daring style showed much of a woman's leg. For dressier occasions, poodle skirts were the first choice for many young U.S. women. Crinolines caused these skirts to flare out, showing off the poodle sewn toward the bottom of the skirt. The short socks and running shoes that often accompanied poodle skirts made the outfit comfortable and easy to move around in. Hair tied back in a ponytail with a ribbon finished off the teen look. Some older women preferred straighter styles. Tight-fitting skirts with tailor-fitted jackets were an important part of a woman's wardrobe. Short gloves were often worn to accent the classy outfits.

1954
Cecil Beaton's "The Glass of Fashion" is published, describing the history of style.

1955
Traditional Japanese, Turkish, and Indian styles influence western fashion.

Guys Liven Up

1950s

Guys Liven Up

For the first time, pink became popular. It had always appeared on women's undergarments or dresses, but it had never been introduced into men's wardrobes. In the fifties, the traditional men's charcoal gray suits gave way to color. Pink ties and hatbands began to creep into closets across the country. Freed from their fashion prisons, men took advantage of the new styles. They wore Bermuda shorts and sported thin Colonel ties to shake up suits. High school students went back to school in pleated rogue pants. These pants had a white stripe along the side and were often worn with a matching white belt. Boys and men also bought closets full of baggy pegged pants to wear to dance hall sock hops.

1954

Davy Crockett Style

On December 15, 1954, Walt Disney's weekly television show Disneyland created hysteria with young people. Children could not get enough of Davy Crockett. Fess Parker starred as the lovable Davy Crockett—and kicked off a $100 million market for his coonskin hats. Many children between 5 and 15 years old had to have an authentic coonskin cap. Stores could not keep enough Davy Crockett lunch boxes, caps, T-shirts, bathing suits, and even guitars on the shelves. An album called The Ballad of Davy Crockett sold 4 million copies. Davy Crockett was

Davy Crockett Style

1956

Capes rather than coats are often worn over dresses and gowns.

1957

Christian Dior dies, passing the business to assistant Yves Saint Laurent.

Head-to-Toe Fashion

everywhere, but only for a while. By the summer of 1955, the Davy Crockett phase had fizzled, leaving stores with boxes of unsold items.

1957

Head-to-Toe Fashion

Both men and women brought new hairstyles to the fifties fashion scene. Many men often went with the ducktail style. This haircut required that one side be folded into the other,

much like a duck's tail. Hollywood stars made this hairdo a must. The style was a fad, but not everyone liked it. In February 1957, a Massachusetts school stopped allowing its students to wear their hair in a ducktail. Crewcuts or flattops, on the other hand, were steady favorites with young and old. The military-inspired style was short and squared off at the sides. Parents approved of this clean-cut fashion. Women also introduced new hairstyles in the fifties. The poodle was worn by both young and mature women. This short hairstyle was permed into tight curls—much like a poodle's curly locks.

Hollywood stars such as Peggy Ann Garner, Ann Sothern, and Faye Emerson, helped make this look popular. Other women preferred longer, straighter styles. It took great efforts to make the ends of their hair curl upwards. With their heads looking great, Americans looked for new styles for the feet. Late in the decade, stiletto heels became popular. These shoes had pointed heels and narrow toes. Despite protests from doctors, who said these shoes could harm feet, and from flooring specialists, who blamed stilettos for dents and holes in carpets and wood floors, many Americans insisted on having at least one pair of these shoes. Sensible saddle shoes and penny loafers remained popular throughout the decade.

Into the Future

Children across the United States often enjoy dressing up as their heroes, just as children in the 1950s copied Davy Crockett. Crockett merchandise would be sold again, years later, to fans of the show. Think about the television shows you watch today. Would you like to dress like the people on these shows? Do you think these same fashions will be in style years from now?

1958
Fur is often used as trim or lining on coats and jackets.

1959
TV versions of 1930s movies influence fashion trends.

1960
Mattel begins selling Barbie, the U.S.'s first fashion doll.

Fashion
1940s

Fashion Led by War

The war interfered with forties fashions. U.S. designers based many of their fashions on military uniforms. The "Eisenhower" jacket had shoulder pads and a drawstring waist. Berets and army hats were a hit with women. As the war dragged on, there was a shortage of material, so hemlines rose to save on fabric. Since metal used to make zippers was needed for the war, designers met the challenge with wraparound skirts. Fashion kept up with women's lifestyles. Women across the country were working, so the dresses and formal suits in their wardrobes were no longer practical. Casual clothing became popular, and short hair was all the rage. Women kept their hair short because long hair got in the way when they were working in factories. Short hair was still feminine, because many women kept their curls and waves intact. Those who chose to keep their hair long often pulled it back with a scarf or piled it on top of their head. Once the war was finally over, many women were eager for feminine, shapely styles again.

Fashion Led by War

1941	1942	1943
Aerosol cans are patented. They are soon used for hair spray.	Cloth is rationed during the war.	Wartime restrictions limit the amounts of wool and silk that are allowed in garments.

Young Fashions

pictures of hearts, flowers, and horses on their jeans. Boys who did not wear army boots often liked to show off their loafers with their jeans rolled up a few inches, too. Boys and girls wore their shirts baggy and rarely tucked in. Some boys wore their letterman jackets or cardigans to show their school and team pride. Another fashion craze was striped football socks. These thick, knee-high socks worn by football players were a must with a skirt and loafers. Other teenagers wore mismatched shoes and socks as a fashion statement. For going out on dates, girls dressed up. They wore Stadium Girl lipstick and make-up, and looked to the many teen magazines for advice.

1940s

New Duds for Men

At the end of the war, men's styles changed dramatically. Many soldiers who had returned to the U.S. had changed a great deal, too. They had left home as boys, and they came home as men, with bodies that would not fit into their old clothes. As troops were demobilized, the government gave each soldier a civilian suit to wear. These were dubbed "demob suits." Each man also was given a tie, a shirt, shoes, and a raincoat in which to re-enter civilian life. Some did not like the suits. They criticized the quality and insisted they were too boxy to be fashionable. Despite this, many men continued to wear demob suits for many years after the war.

1940s

Young Fashions

Young people borrowed some fashions from the military. Many young men would not leave the house without their army boots. Boys and girls chose blue jeans, a necessity for defense workers. They liked the jeans baggy, and many girls rolled the pant legs up to just below their knees. Some girls even painted

New Duds for Men

Pedal Pushers

Pedal Pushers

In the forties, most young people wore pants because of their factory and war jobs. Fashion designers changed their styles to fit this trend and other new habits. Teenagers often got around town on bicycles. Flowing skirts were impractical and a nuisance while on a bike. The rise of this hobby changed how some teens dressed. Pants called "pedal pushers" became popular in the forties. Pedal pushers were mid-calf length— they were either cut that length or rolled up. They were often worn with ankle socks rolled down. Pedal pushers made bicycle riding easier because the pants did not get caught in the sprocket or chain. The style was light and fun, something Americans were looking for during the war years. While teens started this fad, adults followed their lead throughout the decade. Pedal pushers were worn well into the 1950s by adults as well as teens.

1941

Fashionable Science

A breakthrough in science led to a fashion must in the 1940s. A synthesized material called nylon had been created in 1934. By 1939, nylon stockings were being produced. These nylons had a seam running down the back of the leg. In the first year, 64 million pairs of nylons were sold to U.S women. There were near-riots in stores as women scrambled to get a pair for themselves. The war made nylon a rare find. Many U.S. women adapted to the shortage and drew a seam down the back of their bare legs to give the illusion of nylons. Other advancements in fabric soon followed. In 1941, scientists invented an amazing fiber called Terylene. When woven, knitted, or blended with wool or cotton, this fabric would not stretch, fade, wrinkle, or get eaten by insects. After the war, Du Pont brought the fabric to the U.S. as Dacron.

Fashionable Science

1946
The bikini bathing suit debuts.

1947
Dior returns to longer lengths and fuller skirts. This is dubbed the "New Look."

1948
American women protest European designers' use of longer hemlines.

New Looks

After the war, many American women craved a fashion that would recognize their femininity. In 1947, designer Christian Dior shook off the remnants of years of war style with his "New Look." The hemlines that had been forced up because of rationing were let down again. The look was elegant—long flowing skirts, narrow-shouldered jackets, and tight waistlines. After years of wearing coveralls and men's styles, this softer look celebrated femininity. No woman's wardrobe was complete without at least one "New Look" outfit. Dior's design house continued to set fashion trends for more than fifty-five years.

New Looks

Into the Future

The wartime era had a huge effect on the fashion of the 1940s. During the war, resources were scarce. Most Americans did their part to help by saving material and fabric. Think about your life today, and ways that you would be able to make do with less?

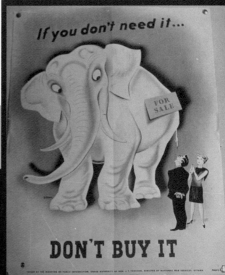

If you don't need it...

FOR SALE

DON'T BUY IT

1949
Women pin fake flowers to lapels and belts.

1950
Hazel Bishop manufactures and sells her kiss-proof lipstick for $1 per tube.

33

Fashion
1930s

What to Wear
Ginger Rogers
and Fred Astaire

What to Wear

Styles in the thirties brought back a woman's shape. Fabrics draped over her shoulders and dresses were cut to show off her back. Evening clothes and day clothes became more distinctly separated— daywear was conservative, often made up of two-piece outfits. Skirt lengths crept up to mid-calf or higher as the decade passed. To go out to the nightclubs, women wore long gowns and men wore tuxedos. Some women caused scandals by showing their midriffs in evening dresses. Fred Astaire and Ginger Rogers were the ideal that many Americans were trying to imitate when they dressed for a night out. Clothing was often in dark, neutral colors. Some designers tried to rock the boat by introducing vibrant colors, including hot pink. This brightness was shocking to many. Women did not commonly wear it. However, society slowly began to accept brighter colors, and colorful clothes were introduced into women's closets across the country. Patterns were also introduced. Floral as well as abstract prints were popular during the thirties.

1931
Ellery Chun designs the first Hawai'ian aloha shirt.

1932
Charles and Joseph Revson found the Revlon company.

Fashion Changes

The stock market crash affected all segments of American life, including fashion. Before the Depression, people often changed clothes several times during the day. That came to an end. Little money meant no new clothing budget. People wore their old clothes for longer to save money and patched or mended them rather than buying new. Also, women made their family's clothing to save money. Going-out-of-business sales became common, as limited budgets drove tailors and clothing stores to bankruptcy. To try to survive the tough times, clothing sellers brought prices down, making fashion more affordable for everyday Americans.

Fashion Changes

1933	1934	1935
Rene Lacoste founds the Lacoste clothing company.	Wallace Carothers manufactures the first nylon polymer.	Pancake makeup is invented to make skin appear natural on color film.

Thirties Man

The style of men's clothing changed during the 1930s. In the early thirties, men's suits were made to create the illusion of a large upper body. Shoulder pads or wadding were used to square off the shoulders, and sleeves were tight to the wrists. Lapels were peaked, which added width to the already wide shoulders and framed the chest. The double-breasted suit also became popular during the thirties. Jackets were long, lapels were wide, and buttons were everywhere. There were often up to eight buttons on a double-breasted jacket. Pants were long and comfortable. This classy style was made mostly in dark colors—charcoal, gray, slate, and midnight or navy blue. The dark fabrics often had stripes worked into them. Brown accents were popular in the winter and white, red, or blue silk accents were popular in the spring. Every man at this time needed a striped suit in his wardrobe, whether wide, narrow, single or double stripes. Checks on suits were another style option for men in the thirties. Thirties society also affected fashion. The way gangsters dressed found its way into mainstream society. This influence brought the extreme styles to American men. Gangsters wore bolder plaids, wider stripes, and colorful ties. The shoulders were even broader, the waists even narrower, and the pant legs even wider. Many gangsters personalized their outfits by embroidering their initials on the pockets or shirt fronts. To top the look, gangsters wore felt hats in shades of green, lilac, blue, brown, and gray. Men rushed to the stores to imitate this rebellious style.

Thirties Man

1936
Yves Saint Laurent is born.

1937
Tight sweaters become a popular look for young women.

1938
Men wear padded shoulders and wide lapels.

Curves Ahead

The twenties women had leaned toward boxy, boyish styles. In the thirties, feminine styles were back in fashion. Necklines dipped and were surrounded by ruffles and scalloped edges to draw attention to them. Finally, waistlines returned to where they naturally fell on a woman. Skirts were full, making a woman with a small waist and minimal hips a vision of fashionability. Ruffled skirts, sometimes in tiers, appeared on store racks for the first time. Headwear changed as well. Hats were worn at an angle and tiny pillbox hats were just as popular as traditional brimmed hats. Fur coats, stoles, and wraps were popular items of both day and evening wear with the upper classes. Whether wealthy or struggling, many women looked past the racks to the silver screen to decide what they should wear. Hollywood stars endorsed styles and made certain accessories popular just by wearing them in their movies. Throughout the thirties, women tried to mimic the styles they saw movie stars wearing in their favorite films.

Curves Ahead

Into the Future

The Great Depression left people in the 1930s with little money to spend on clothing. They had to repair old clothes rather than buying new ones. Can you think of ways to recycle your clothes so that they can be used for a long time? Are there ways to update older items so that they look like modern trends?

1939

Levi Strauss & Co. make the red pocket tab its official trademark.

1940

Nylon stockings first become available for purchase in the United States.

Fashion
1920s

Men's Closets

After World War I, American men returned home to closets full of clothing they had worn as teenagers. They traded in their army fatigues and dress uniforms for the sack suit. During the day, men wore these suits with colored shirts and silk ties of various patterns. Bowler hats topped off the perfect day outfit. For evening wear, elegant twenties' men wore jackets with tails. Tuxedos were slowly gaining popularity at high-society functions. For casual wear, American men wore lace-up two-toned shoes, often in white and tan, and many wore knickers—loose-fitting short pants gathered at the knee.

Men's Closets

1921
Guccio Gucci opens his first store in Florence.

1922
Madeleine Vionnet begins designing clothes that would become trendy in the

Free-Spirited Fashion

women. Gone were the days of showing off curves. Boyish figures and bobbed haircuts were in style, and clothes were chosen to hide any curves. Flappers led the fashion revolution. They wore outfits that were baggy and short. The dresses were often sleeveless and their bare arms created scandals. Their stockings were turned down, exposing powdered knees.

1920s

Oxford Bags

At many university campuses, young men were not allowed to wear knickers. To get around this restriction, many turned to Oxford bags. These pants were between 22 and 40 inches wide around the bottom. Students could wear their knickers before and after class and slip the Oxford bags over them while in class.

1920s

Free-Spirited Fashion

The twenties was a decade of happy-go-lucky attitudes encouraged by prosperity. Women's waistlines moved from the natural waist down to between the waist and the hips—and then disappeared altogether. Clothing was loose and unrestricted, much like the lifestyles of many American

Oxford Bags

1923
Shoemaker Salvatore Ferragamo's one-of-a-kind creations are seen on movie stars.

1924
The popularity of rayon fabric reduces demand for cotton.

1925
Flapper fashion is in full swing.

Swim Style

Before World War I, women had worn bathing dresses to swim in. These elaborate outfits even included bloomers. After the war, designers showcased modern bathing suit styles. These early styles consisted of form-fitting tank tops pulled down and belted over short woolen shorts.

And the Winner

In 1921, eight women battled for the title of Miss America. It was the first time the beauty pageant had been held. Atlantic City had little tourism after Labor Day. The pageant was seen as a way to draw more people to the city in the fall. The contest was hosted

And the Winner

by an unlikely person—a wealthy inventor, Hudson Maxim, who had made his fortune in explosives. The Miss America pageant was explosive as well! It featured a "bathing revue," during which even the men in the orchestra wore swimsuits. Sixteen-year-old Margaret Gorman was crowned the first Miss America. While many people scoffed at the contest, it fitted well with the ideas and tastes of the Jazz Age. The following year, a total of fifty-seven cities sent women to represent them at the Miss America pageant.

Swim Style

1926
Hemlines reach a new high, rising to the knee for the first time.

1927
Elsa Schiaparelli launches a new line, selling uniquely tailored clothes in wild colors and styles.

1928
The clip-on tie is designed.

1921

Crazy for Coco

In 1914, Coco Chanel opened a hat shop in Paris, France. By 1921, the French woman's name was associated with style and elegance. She introduced a new perfume called Chanel No. 5, which became the most successful perfume ever produced. Chanel also introduced a line of clothing that was simple and elegant, just like her perfume. Every wealthy American woman had her closets stocked with Chanel's tweed suits, jersey blouses, trench coats, turtleneck sweaters, and her "little black dress." Chanel's suits—a collarless cardigan and a skirt—have been imitated for decades.

Crazy for Coco

Into the Future

In the 1920s, rules and suggestions about what could be worn were much more strict than they are today. Over time, fashion tends to accept what is considered less stylish at first. Think about unusual clothing styles you have seen. Do you think any of these styles might some day be accepted in mainstream fashion?

1929

San Francisco police detain a woman for dressing in men's clothing.

1930

Following the stock market crash, the Sears Catalogue states, "thrift is the spirit of the day."

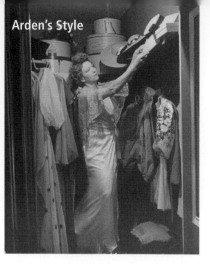

Arden's Style

1910s

Dandy Gentlemen

In the early 1910s, designers created new looks for men. The most fashionable men wore one- or three-button coat or a double-breasted straight-hanging jacket. Pants became wider, measuring about 22 inches around the bottom of the pant legs. Men wanted to look "dandy." To dress up for the evening, a fashionable man carried a cane and wore a high-collared jacket set off with a bow tie. To finish off the look, a bowler or other style of hat was a must. Younger men and boys often wore three-piece suits for evenings out. The pants fitted the wearer snugly and had reinforced or double knees. High stockings met the bottom of the pants so no skin showed.

1910s

Arden's Style

In 1910, Elizabeth Arden opened a beauty salon with a bright red door as an invitation. The salon was on ritzy Fifth Avenue. Her salon was incredibly successful, so she opened more stores. The red door became a symbol of quality cosmetics that were very "ladylike." She soon released a makeup line that came to boast more than 300 items. By the time of her death in 1966, Elizabeth Arden was a fashion legend with more than 100 salons carrying her name.

1910s

Tight-fitting Fashions

In the 1900s, women wore tight undergarments called corsets that pinched and made breathing difficult. In the 1910s, they discarded these pieces of clothing. The bodices that replaced them were similar to corsets but looser and bloused out. This gave clothing a more natural look. For the first time, women's comfort was considered when determining the latest fashions. In 1912, other fashion restrictions appeared on store racks. Skirts were designed to fit very tightly at the ankle. By 1914, skirt-bottoms were so tight that women could barely walk. Fashionable women were forced to take tiny, stuttered steps—that was all the material would allow. Designers began adding slits and pleats in the fabric. This gave the

Dandy Gentlemen

Tight-fitting Fashions

1911
The "lampshade" tunic gains popularity.

1914
The first American fashion show is held.

1915
Lipstick is first sold in tubes.

appearance of a narrow style while allowing women to walk with a more normal stride. Even with these improvements, the dresses were impractical. Stepping up to a streetcar or even climbing stairs became an incredible challenge.

1910s

Headwear

Women in the 1910s began cropping their hair in bobs. During the war, female factory workers found longer hair a nuisance. While many younger women chose shorter styles, others kept the curls made famous by the actress Mary Pickford. Women who wore their hair short used fancy combs, hairpins, barrettes, and other clips to accent an outfit or to pull their hair back with style. Traditional longer hairstyles were often worn piled on top of the head under a hat or gathered in a twist at the nape of the neck. Headgear was an important item. The finishing touch to evening wear was a beautiful headpiece. Some women used strips of material studded with jewels to match their evening gowns. These hair bands resembled crowns or tiaras, and they were often trimmed with a feather. In 1912, dancer Irene Castle introduced U.S. women to embroidered caps. They became a fashion necessity. Most women had several hats, suitable for various occasions.

1910s

Straight Style

Before the 1910s, dresses often had extra material bustled down the back. Now dresses flowed smoothly and hung softly over women's bodies. Dresses were also almost completely straight. The most eye-catching feature of the new look was the length of the dresses. Day dresses were shorter, exposing the wearer's ankle. Some were even a few inches above the ankle. Younger women loved the revolutionary fashions and bought straight dresses in droves. Men also enjoyed the straighter styles. The days of over-starched, crisp suit shirts were over. Shoulder pads were removed from jackets to allow the jacket to fall straighter on the body. Suits and jackets became more fitted, and comfort became a consideration for men as well. Men even abandoned their lace-up boots for soft, comfortable oxford shoes.

Straight Style

Headwear

1916

Women working in factories during World War I begin wearing slacks on a regular basis.

1919

American women wear full boots less often in favor of pumps.

43

Hairy Situation

1900s

Hairy Situation

Permanents, or perms, were first introduced in 1906. To achieve permanent waves, women had to pay dearly. The technique cost $1,000 and took eight to twelve hours to complete. Women who could not spend so much money on a hairstyle turned to the pompadour. Hair was combed high off the forehead and then piled on top of the head. This style, also called Gibson Girl hair and the psyche knot, was very popular. French twists and smaller, more controlled styles were often worn, too. Men followed fashion trends as well. By the beginning of the century, many men traded their large mustaches and beards for clean shaves. However, a wide variety of styles were available for men of the 1900s. Some men preferred well-groomed mustaches and small

beards. Facial hair was controlled and styled using wax. Sideburns continued to be popular, but they were shorter than in previous decades. Some men chose to wear muttonchops and chin beards trimmed to a point. Still others kept the longer, bushier mustaches.

1900s

Unnatural Posture

The "health corset" hit the market in 1900. Along with some extra fabric at the back, this corset gave women's bodies an S-shape. Dressing in the 1900s was a complicated business. Women wore many layers of clothing every day, regardless of the temperature. They first put on underlayers of the dress, belts, drawers, linings for the skirt, and a rigid layer or boning to give dresses their shape. Then came petticoats, which added volume to the dress. Extra fabric, called a bustle, was added to women's backsides to achieve the "S" effect. Their upper bodies were hidden under corsets and vests. These vests created the top arc of

Unnatural Posture

1900	1904
Annie Turnbo develops and begins selling a line of hair products.	Pope Pius X bans the wearing of low-cut dresses around churchmen.

Sacrifice for Style

the "S," and the fabric, petticoats, liners, and boning created the bottom arc. Many women were relieved to see this style loosen up in 1907.

1900s

Sacrifice for Style

At the beginning of the century, women's fashions followed the trends of the previous decade. Fashionable women wore tightly fitted corsets under layers of decorative fabric. One purpose of a woman's wardrobe was to show her father's or husband's wealth and status. As a result, only wealthy women had the time and money to follow the

latest trends and own the most stylish hats and petticoats. Middle-class women copied the fashions they saw in magazines and newspapers. They showed styles to dressmakers to reproduce, or sewed their own versions of the day's look. As the decade progressed, fashion began to change. The fresh ideas of Parisian designer Paul Poiret brought a new look to American women. The S-shape gave way to Poiret's straight, high-waisted classical styles. By 1908, the Straight Line allowed dresses to fall around the body in a narrow column. Designs were more natural—and more comfortable. Still, Poiret's designs had their faults. His clothes required a different type of corset that reached the knees. Standing was easy, but sitting down posed some challenges. Later, Poiret designed the narrow hobble skirt, which made walking difficult.

1900s

The Price of Fashion

In 1900, women's styles became less ornamented. Designers experimented with two-piece outfits that had high necks and tight sleeves. Bustles were abandoned for smoother lines. American women were expected to fit a specific mold. Those who

did not fit it tried to squeeze their bodies into shape by using corsets. Paris fashion designers stated that 18 inches was the perfect waist measurement. Women around the world fainted while trying to cinch themselves into corsets to fit this standard. Dresses were tight to the hip and flared wide at the bottom to hide a woman's real shape. Respectable women did not show any skin on their arms or neck, so many women were covered in fabric, even in the heat of summer. Women who played sports had to do so in skirts that reached their ankles. Even bathing suits, which were seen as short and revealing, reached the mid-calf. Women were not the only ones to cover up. Now that mixed-gender public swimming was popular, men had to cover their chests. Men's swimsuits were made up of a tank shirt and shorts.

The Price of Fashion

1905
Fashion designer Christian Dior is born.

1906
The Converse Shoe Company is founded.

1909
Bobbed hair becomes fashionable.

ACTIVITY
Into the future

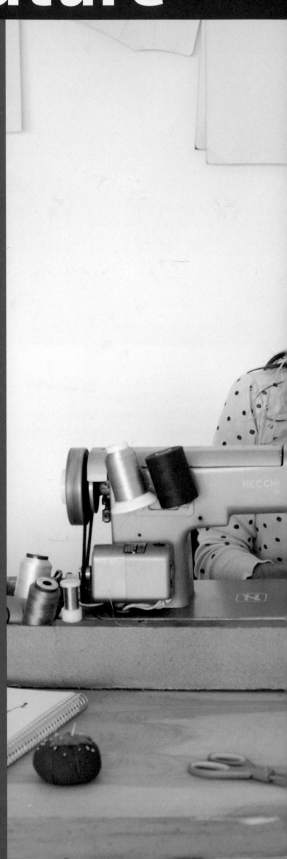

Fashion is affected by many things and changes rapidly. It is difficult to predict which direction fashion may take in the future, but many people make a career of trying to determine what will be the next trend. Fashion designers use their experience, **intuition**, and artistic sense to develop new styles. Not everything they design is a success, but sometimes, a new innovation can really become popular. The bikini, bell-bottom pants, and Chuck Taylor sneakers are all examples of ideas that have achieved great popularity.

What would you design if you were one of the world's fashion leaders? A successful fashion designer must have a sense of current trends in fashion and strong opinions about style. Every designer has influences that affect how he or she thinks about style. What are your influences? What styles do you like, and what fashions seem silly or boring to you? Focus on fashion that you find most exciting.

Some designers produce many different clothing items, such as dresses, suits, shoes, and accessories. Others specialize in only one or two items. Would you prefer to create and entire look or just some of the elements that make up a great outfit? Next, think about colors, shapes, and markets. Who will you design this item for—men, women, children?

Become a Designer

Once you have decided what you would like to design, try making a sample of your product. First, lightly draw the figure of a person who will be wearing your new fashion trend. Once you have a figure on your paper, you can begin to add clothing or accessories that fit naturally with the human form. Be sure to show all of the details of the design. Next, you can try drawing the design from different angles. When you are finished, share your results with your friends. Every successful designer needs input and advice from the public. Make adjustments to your design based on what they say.

FURTHER
Research

Many books and websites provide information about fashion. To learn more about this topic, borrow books from the library, or surf the Internet.

Books

Most libraries have computers that connect to a database for researching information. If you input a key word, you will be provided with a list of books in the library that contain information on that topic. Non-fiction books are arranged numerically, using their call number. Fiction books are organized alphabetically by the author's last name.

Websites

For more information about fashion, visit **www.pbs.org/newshour/infocus/fashion/whatisfashion.html**.

For news about fashion, surf to **www.style.com**.

Glossary

asymmetrical: having parts that are different or unequal

corset: a tightly fitting undergarment for women

demobilized: disbanded after war

Great Depression: an era when the economy was in great decline; beginning in 1929 and lasting through the 1930s

icon: a symbol or representative

individuality: the features of a certain person that make him or her stand out from others

lapel: the part of a coat or jacket below the collar that is folded over on each side of the opening

muttonchops: men's facial worn in the shape of a meat chop; having a large round bottom and narrow top

polyester: a human-made fabric

revolution: a widespread change in the way something is viewed or done

utilitarian: something that is useful instead of attractive

versatility: the ability to be used for many things

vintage: something that was produced in a different year

vogue: the top fashions of a certain time period

waifish: like a helpless person or abandoned child

Index

bathing suits 28, 32, 40, 45
Beatles, The 23, 24, 25
Beckham, Victoria 7

corset 42, 44, 45

denim 15
designers 5, 6, 11, 12, 13, 14, 15, 19, 20, 25, 30, 31, 32, 33, 34, 40, 43, 45, 46
disco 12, 16, 18, 19, 20, 21, 25
dresses 10, 19, 20, 24, 26, 27, 28, 30, 34, 39, 40, 41, 43, 44, 45, 46

fitness 14, 16, 20

Great Depression 35, 37

hairstyle 11, 12, 17, 21, 22, 23, 28, 29, 43, 44
hats 41, 42, 43
hip-hop 5, 8, 11, 13, 25

Lopez, Jennifer 8, 9

Madonna 14

suits 6, 8, 10, 18, 19, 23, 27, 28, 30, 21, 32, 36, 38, 41, 42, 43, 46

Twiggy 24

wars 4, 26, 30, 31, 32, 33, 38, 40, 43